50 CREATURES

An Adult Coloring Book

Chloe Sky

P&K Publications, LLC

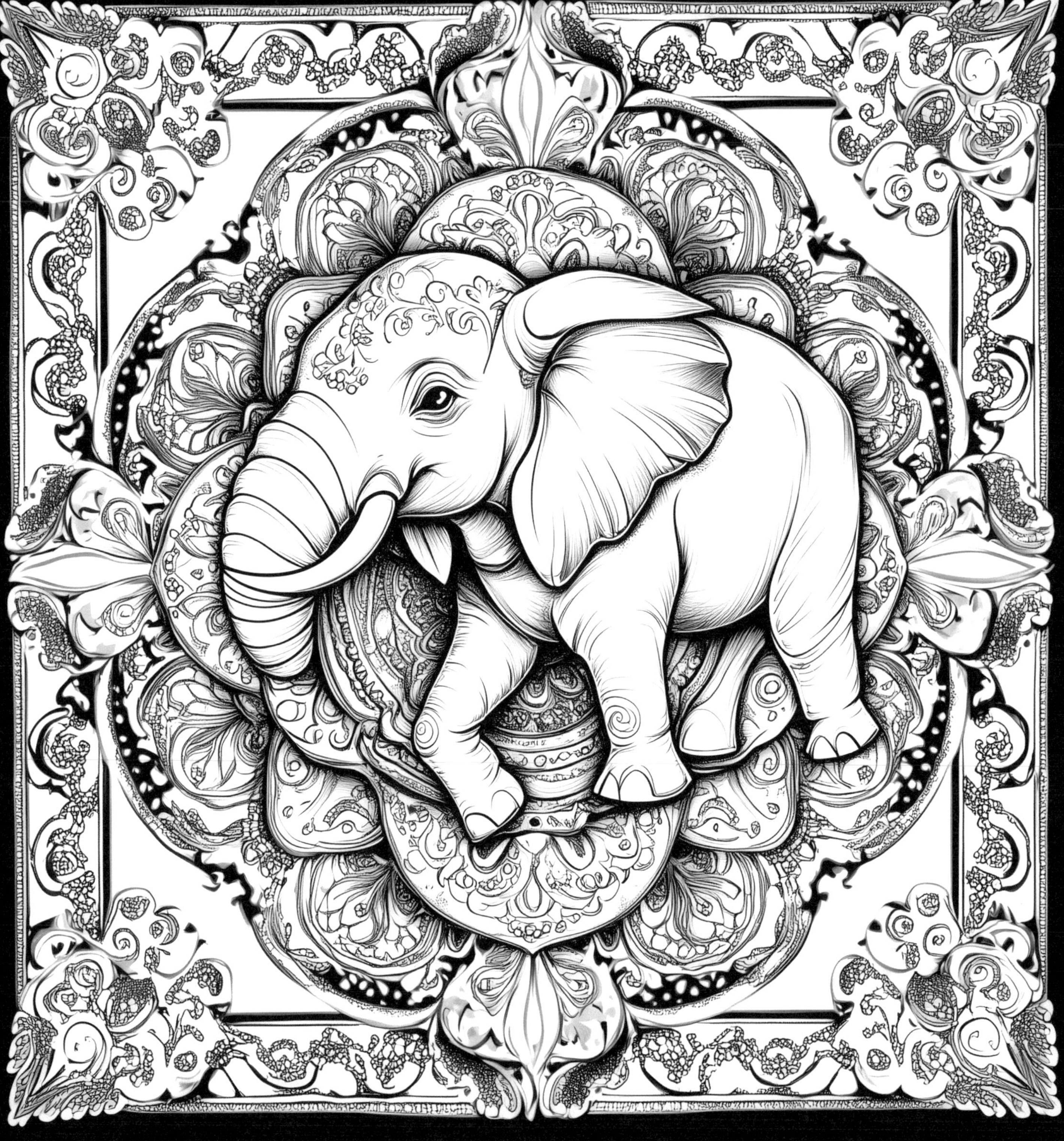

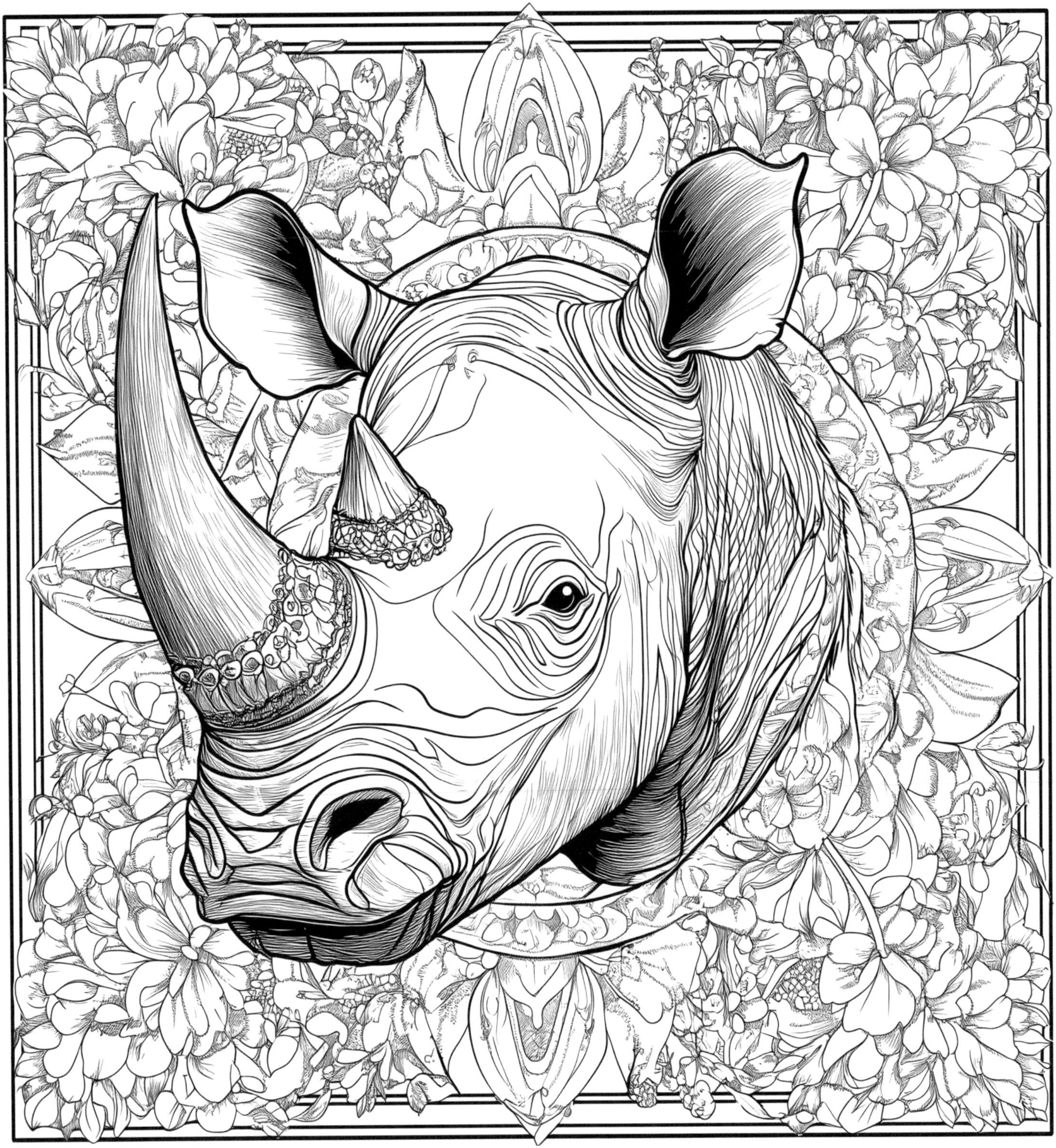

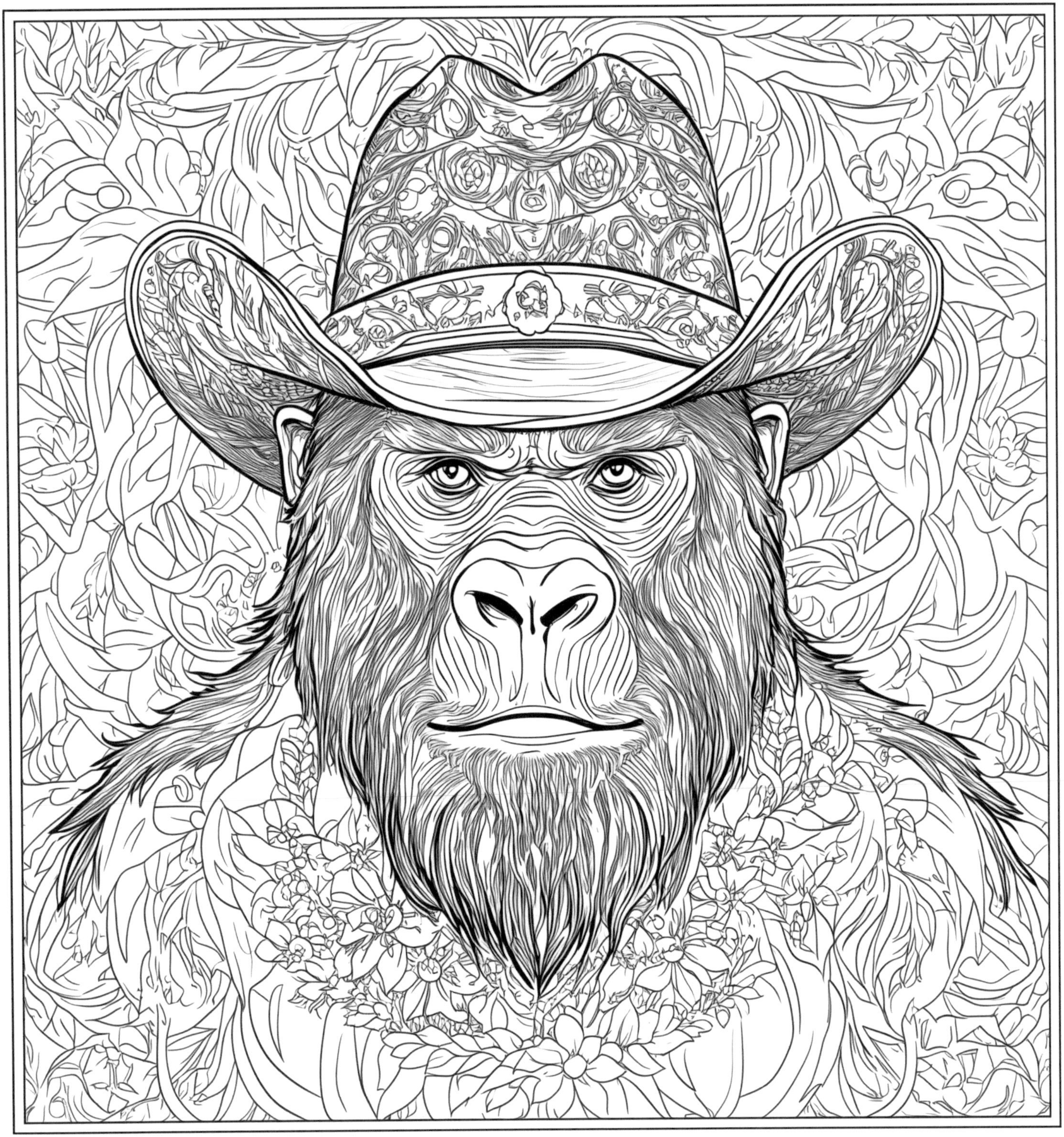

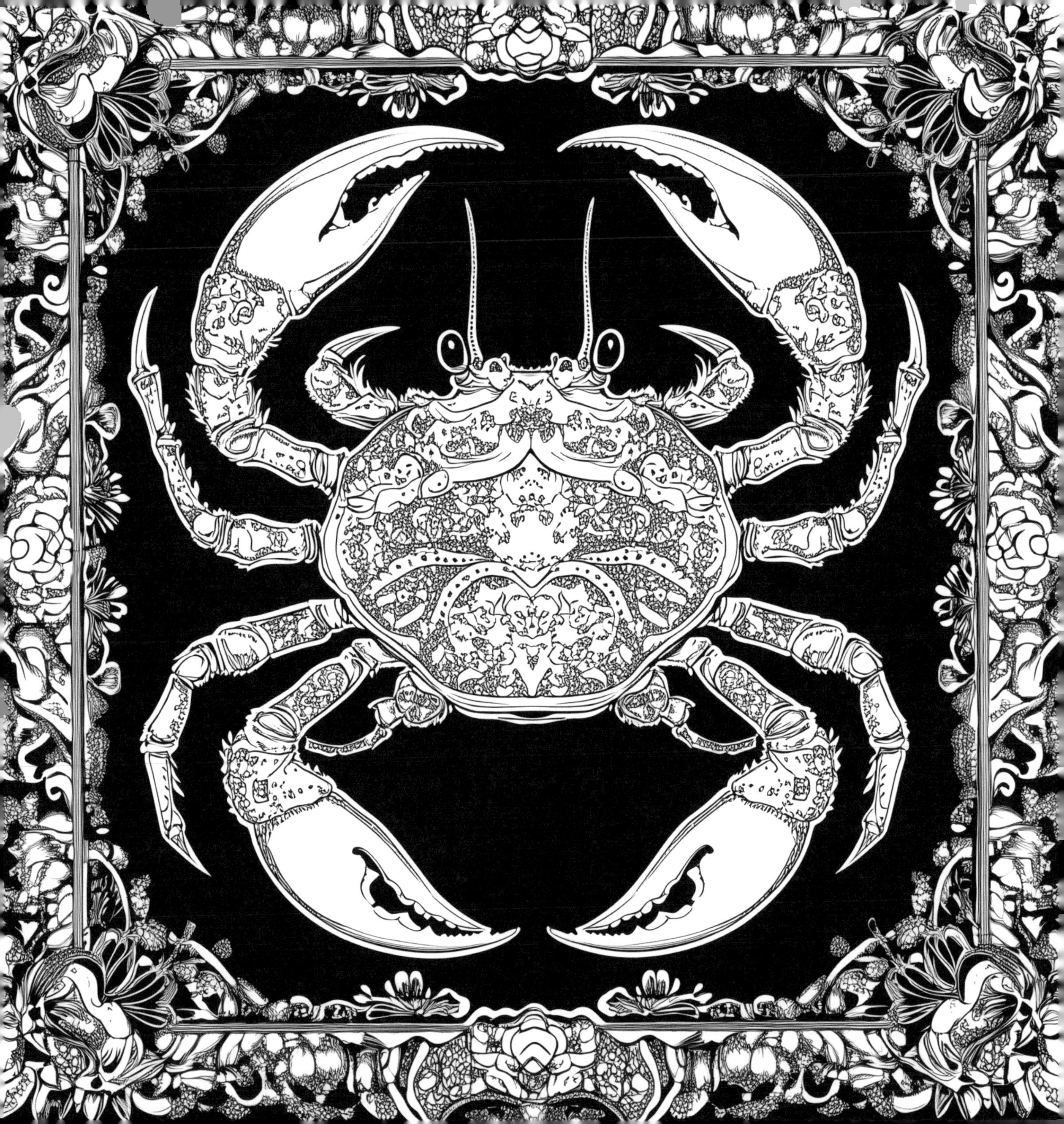

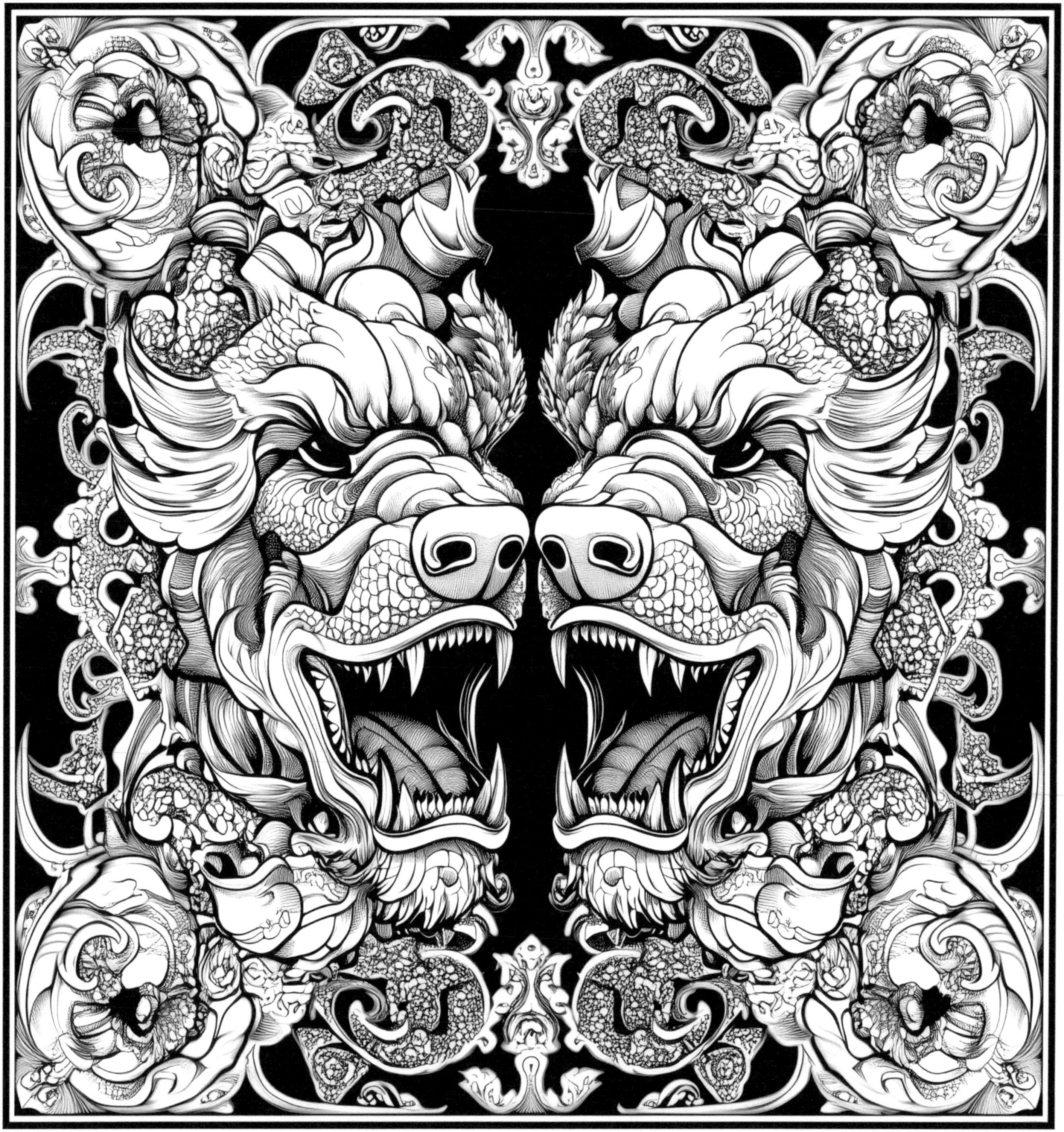

Made in the USA
Thornton, CO
09/21/24 00:14:15

76f923fd-1b0b-4e35-b6f4-66086eb4356eR01